בָּרְכוּ

What kinds of signals tell you something important is about to start? There's the bell announcing that it's time for recess, the ringing telephone meaning that someone wants to talk to you, and the lights going off in the movies telling you that the show is about to begin.

The בָּרְכוּ prayer is a signal—it calls the congregation together, announcing that the main part of the prayer service is about to start.

In many congregations the leader of the service says the first line of the בָּרְכוּ while bowing as a sign of respect to God—the same way one might bow down toward a king or a queen. The congregation recites the second line of the prayer in response while bowing, too.

Practice reading the בָּרְכוּ aloud.

1. בָּרְכוּ אֶת־יְיָ הַמְבֹרָךְ.
2. בָּרוּךְ יְיָ הַמְבֹרָךְ לְעוֹלָם וָעֶד.

Praise Adonai, who is to be praised.
Praised is Adonai, who is to be praised forever and ever.

PRAYER DICTIONARY

בָּרְכוּ
praise!

יְיָ
Adonai

הַמְבֹרָךְ
who is to be praised

בָּרוּךְ
praised, blessed

לְעוֹלָם וָעֶד
forever and ever

SEARCH AND CIRCLE

Circle the Hebrew word(s) that means the same as the English.

forever and ever	בָּרְכוּ לְעוֹלָם וָעֶד אֶת
Adonai	יְיָ בָּרְכוּ בָּרוּךְ
praise!	בָּרְכוּ הַמְבֹרָךְ אֶת
who is to be praised	אֶת לְעוֹלָם וָעֶד הַמְבֹרָךְ

MATCH GAME

Connect the Hebrew word(s) to the English meaning.

who is to be praised   בָּרְכוּ

Adonai   יְיָ

praise!   הַמְבֹרָךְ

forever and ever   בָּרוּךְ

praised, blessed   לְעוֹלָם וָעֶד

WHAT'S MISSING?

Complete each prayer phrase with the missing Hebrew word(s).

אֶת יְיָ הַמְבֹרָךְ. _____ praise!

בָּרוּךְ יְיָ הַמְבֹרָךְ _____ _____. forever and ever

בָּרְכוּ אֶת _____ הַמְבֹרָךְ. Adonai

יְיָ הַמְבֹרָךְ לְעוֹלָם וָעֶד. _____ praised

FAMILY LETTERS

The words below contain family letters: ךככ and בב.
Practice reading them.

1. כך   מֶלֶךְ   כָּל   לָךְ   תּוֹכֵנוּ   יָדְךָ   כָּמוֹךָ

2. כּכ   כֹּל   אָכַל   מִכָּל   כָּמֹכָה   כְּמַלְכֵּנוּ   מְכַלְכֵּל

3. בב   בְּבֵית   מַכַּבִּי   בַּלֵּבָב   בִּדְבָרוֹ   כּוֹכָבִים   אֲבָל

3

IN THE SYNAGOGUE

How did the בָּרְכוּ get its name? בָּרְכוּ is the first word of the prayer. The first word of a Hebrew prayer is often the name by which the prayer is known.

The בָּרְכוּ is thousands of years old. The Jewish people have said the בָּרְכוּ since the time of the Temple—בֵּית הַמִּקְדָּשׁ. Today, in many congregations the leader of the service calls us to pray with the very same words that were recited in the Temple.

The cantor or rabbi chants

בָּרְכוּ אֶת־יְיָ הַמְבֹרָךְ.

and the congregation answers

בָּרוּךְ יְיָ הַמְבֹרָךְ לְעוֹלָם וָעֶד.

Just as we respond to a friendly "hello" with a greeting, we answer the בָּרְכוּ—the Call to Prayer—with the response that yes, we will pray.

ROOTS

Three words in the בָּרְכוּ look and sound similar.

בָּרוּךְ   הַמְבֹרָךְ   בָּרְכוּ

Which three letters appear in each word? ____ ____ ____

(Hint: כּ כ ךְ and בּ ב are family letters.)

> Most Hebrew words are built on roots.
>
> A root usually consists of three letters that form the foundation for new, related words.
>
> A root has no vowels.
>
> The three words above share the root ברכ.
>
> The root ברכ means "bless" or "praise."

Circle the three root letters in each of these words:

הַמְבֹרָךְ   בָּרְכוּ   בָּרוּךְ

Write the root. ____ ____ ____

What does the root ברכ mean? _____ _____

FINAL LETTER REVIEW

The words below end in a final letter. Practice reading the words.

1. עֵץ   שָׁלוֹם   בָּרוּךְ   חָמֵץ   נוֹתֵן
2. יוֹסֵף   אַבְרָהָם   מִנְיָן   מֶלֶךְ   אָלֶף

5

DID YOU KNOW?

The בָּרְכוּ is also part of the blessing said before we read from the Torah.

Practice reading the Torah blessing.

1. בָּרְכוּ אֶת־יְיָ הַמְבֹרָךְ.

2. בָּרוּךְ יְיָ הַמְבֹרָךְ לְעוֹלָם וָעֶד.

3. בָּרוּךְ אַתָּה, יְיָ אֱלֹהֵינוּ, מֶלֶךְ הָעוֹלָם,

4. אֲשֶׁר בָּחַר בָּנוּ מִכָּל הָעַמִּים, וְנָתַן לָנוּ אֶת תּוֹרָתוֹ.

5. בָּרוּךְ אַתָּה, יְיָ, נוֹתֵן הַתּוֹרָה.

Why do you think the בָּרְכוּ was made a part of the Torah blessing?

_____

_____

_____

GOD'S NAME

God's true name is a mystery to us. A long time ago, the *kohanim*—the priests who served in the Temple in Jerusalem—knew how to pronounce God's name. But because it was so holy, the High Priest would say God's name only once a year—on Yom Kippur.

Today we are not really sure how God's name was pronounced, so we say Adonai. (Some people say הַשֵׁם—The Name.)

We pronounce God's name יְיָ as אֲדוֹנָי.

God's name is written in many different ways.

In the בָּרְכוּ God's name is written יְיָ.

In other places in the סִדּוּר, and in the Bible (תַּנַ״ךְ), you may see God's name written יְהֹוָה. יְהֹוָה is also pronounced "Adonai."

In other Hebrew books you may see God's name written like this: ה׳.

You will learn other names for God in later lessons.

READING PRACTICE

Practice reading the following sentences. Circle God's name wherever it appears.

1. בָּרְכוּ אֶת־יְיָ הַמְבֹרָךְ.
2. בָּרוּךְ יְיָ הַמְבֹרָךְ לְעוֹלָם וָעֶד.
3. מֵאֵין כָּמוֹךָ, יְהֹוָה, גָּדוֹל אַתָּה וְגָדוֹל שִׁמְךָ בִּגְבוּרָה.
4. כִּי לְךָ ה׳ הַגְּדֻלָּה וְהַגְּבוּרָה וְהַתִּפְאֶרֶת.
5. יְיָ צְבָאוֹת שְׁמוֹ.
6. גָּדוֹל ה׳ וּמְהֻלָּל מְאֹד, וְלִגְדֻלָּתוֹ אֵין חֵקֶר.

FLUENT READING

Practice reading the lines below.

1. בָּרְכוּ אֶת־יְיָ הַמְבֹרָךְ.

2. בָּרוּךְ יְיָ הַמְבֹרָךְ לְעוֹלָם וָעֶד.

3. בָּרוּךְ אַתָּה יְיָ הָאֵל הַקָּדוֹשׁ.

4. יְיָ עֹז לְעַמּוֹ יִתֵּן, יְיָ יְבָרֵךְ אֶת עַמּוֹ בַשָּׁלוֹם.

5. בָּרוּךְ אַתָּה, יְיָ, הַמְבָרֵךְ אֶת עַמּוֹ יִשְׂרָאֵל בַּשָּׁלוֹם.

6. דָּבָר טוֹב וְקַיָּם לְעוֹלָם וָעֶד.

7. תְּהִלּוֹת לְאֵל עֶלְיוֹן, בָּרוּךְ הוּא וּמְבֹרָךְ.

8. יְיָ, צוּרִי וְגֹאֲלִי.

9. בָּרֵךְ עָלֵינוּ, יְיָ אֱלֹהֵינוּ, אֶת הַשָּׁנָה הַזֹּאת.